HEINEMANN STATE STUDIES

Uniquely
New Mexico

Coleen Hubbard

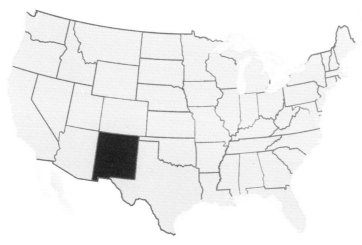

Heinemann Library
Chicago, Illinois

Designed by Heinemann Library
Printed in China by WKT Company Limited.

08 07 06 05 04
10 9 8 7 6 5 4 3 2 1

**Library of Congress
Cataloging-in-Publication Data**

Hubbard, Coleen.
  Uniquely New Mexico / Coleen Hubbard.
    v. cm. — (Heinemann state studies)
  Includes bibliographical references and index.
  Contents: Uniquely New Mexico—New Mexico's
climate—Famous firsts—State symbols—New
Mexico's history and people—Famous people—The
arts of New Mexico—New Mexico's state govern-
ment—New Mexico's culture—New Mexico food—
Folklore and legends—Sports—New Mexico's
businesses and products—Attractions and landmarks.
  ISBN 1-4034-4652-0 (lib. bdg.)—ISBN 1-4034-
4721-7 (pbk.)
  1. New Mexico—Juvenile literature. [1. New
Mexico.] I. Title. II. Series.
  F796.3.H83 2004
  978.9—dc22

                                    2003025447—

Cover Pictures

Top (left to right) New Mexico state flag,
Taos/pueblo-style architecture, Carlsbad
Cavern interior, chilies **Main** Albuquerque
Balloon Festival

Acknowledgments

Development and photo research by
BOOK BUILDERS LLC

The author and publishers are grateful to the
following for permission to reproduce copyright
material:

Cover photographs by (top, L-R): Ron
McQueeney/Artemis Images, Layne Kennedy/
Corbis, Joseph Sohm/Visions of American/Corbis,
Paul Riley/University Athletics, Richard Cummins/
Corbis

Title page (L-R): Robert Harding World Imagery/
Alamy, Tom Till/Alamy, Las Cruces Convention and
Visitor's Bureau; pp. 5, 31T Courtesy of the Las
Cruces Convention and Visitor's Bureau; p. 6 Alan
and Jackie Ellis; p. 8 Philip Lewis/Alamy Images;
pp. 10, 13, 14M, 24B Linda Montoya Images;
p. 14T, 25 Robert Harding World Imagery/Alamy;
p. 14B Ralph Wetmore/Alamy Images; p. 15T Scott
Stulberg/Alamy Images; p. 15B Courtesy Steve
Brusatte/University of Chicago; p; 16T John Blumb/
Alamy Images; p. 16B David Wellington/Animal-
sAnimals; p. 17T Adam Woolfitt/Alamy; p. 18 Tom
Till/Alamy; pp. 19, 20, 21, 26B Culver Pictures;
p. 22 Hulton Archives; p. 23T Courtesy of the
United States Mint; p. 23B Time Life Pictures/Getty
Images; p. 24T Mark Scheuern/Alamy Images;
p. 26T Cary Herz; p. 28, 31B Courtesy New Mex-
ico Department of Tourism; pp. 29, 42T, 42B Andre
Jenny/Alamy Images; p. 30 Layne Kennedy/Corbis;
p 32, 38 Alamy Images; p. 33 StockFood/Silver-
man; pp. 34, 35 R. Capozzelli/Heinemann Library;
p. 36 Matt Dunn/University of New Mexico Media
Relations; p. 37 Dave Benyak/University of New
Mexico Media Relations; p. 39 Getty Images; p. 40
Chad Ehlers/Alamy Images; p. 44 Ernesto Burciaga/
Alamy Images

Special thanks to William Kane from the University
of New Mexico for his expert comments in the
preparation of this book.

Some words are shown in bold, **like this.**
You can find out what they mean by looking
in the glossary.

Contents

Uniquely New Mexico

Being unique means having special qualities that make a person, place, or thing stand out from the crowd. New Mexico is unique in many ways. In 1581 the first road built by Europeans in the present-day United States was completed in what is now New Mexico. It was called *El Camino Real,* which is Spanish for "The Royal Road." Built by Spanish explorers and soldiers, the road connected Mexico City with Santa Fe. In 1948 New Mexico became the first state to give Native American men and women the right to vote in state elections. These are just a few of the things that make New Mexico stand out from the rest.

Origin of the State's Name

The **Aztec** people ruled present-day Mexico from about 1400 until they were defeated by the Spanish in 1519. *Mexico* is an Aztec word meaning "place of Mexitli." Mexitli was the Aztec name for one of those people's gods. Spain then ruled Mexico until Mexico gained its independence in 1823. While in control, in 1561, Spain added the territory to the north, across the Rio Grande. They called this new land *Nuevo Mexico,* or New Mexico. After winning the land in the **U.S.–Mexican War** in 1848, the United States began using the English name.

Major Cities

Santa Fe is the capital of New Mexico. The city, with a population of more than 61,000, is located in the north-central part of the state. Santa Fe is 7,000 feet above sea level, making it the highest state capital in the United States. It is also the oldest capital city in North America and the oldest European community west of the Missis-

Albuquerque hosts the world's largest hot air balloon rally.

sippi River. Santa Fe was founded by the Spanish explorer Don Pedro de Peralta in the early 1600's. It is home to the oldest public building in the United States, the Palace of the Governors built in 1609.

Albuquerque, in central New Mexico, is the largest city in the state. More than 400,000 people live there. In October it hosts the International Balloon Fiesta. For more than a week the skies above the city are filled with thousands of brightly colored hot air balloons. It is also home to the University of New Mexico, the largest school in the state.

Las Cruces is New Mexico's second-largest city. It is the fastest-growing city in the state and the eleventh fastest-growing city in the nation. Located in southern New Mexico, it has about 74,000 residents. Spanish explorer Don Juan de Oñate founded the city in 1598. In 1830 Apache warriors killed Spanish travelers in the area. Their graves were marked with wooden crosses. The name *La Placita de Las Cruces,* or the Place of the Crosses, was shortened to Las Cruces in 1849 and became the settlement's name.

New Mexico's Geography and Climate

New Mexico is the fifth-largest state in the nation. With almost 122,000 square miles, it forms a nearly perfect rectangle with a small "boot heel" at its southwestern corner. The Rio Grande runs down the middle of the state, eventually flowing into the Gulf of Mexico. Even with the Rio Grande, New Mexico has the lowest water-to-land **ratio** in the United States. Lakes and rivers make up only 0.02 percent of the state, so most of the land is dry except when it rains or snows.

LAND

New Mexico has three geographical areas, or regions— the Great Plains, the Rocky Mountains, and the Basin and Range.

The Great Plains covers the eastern third of New Mexico. This is a **semiarid** place, where only a small amount of rain falls each year. The land is flat and covered

Wheeler Peak is the tallest mountain in New Mexico. It is 13,161 feet above sea level.

New Mexico's Dinosaurs

Dinosaurs lived in present-day New Mexico between 75 million and 200 million years ago. Scientists have discovered dinosaur **fossils** in many parts of the state. Plant-eating stegosaurus and allosaurus were the most common dinosaurs in the area. Fossils belonging to seismosaurus, one of the longest dinosaurs, were discovered in northwestern New Mexico in the 1980s. This dinosaur was about as long as half of a football field. Fossils from the seismosaurus can be found in only one place in the world—at the New Mexico Museum of Natural History and Science in Albuquerque.

with short grasses. Mostly it is used for cattle and sheep grazing.

The Rocky Mountains, or the Rockies, cover the northern third of the state. The Rockies stretch from Alaska to New Mexico. The Rio Grande cuts through the mountains from north to south. Most of New Mexico's farms are in the Rio Grande Valley. Next to the Rockies in the east are the Sangre de Cristo Mountains, which come together at Wheeler Peak.

The Basin and Range region is south of the Rockies. This area is south of Sante Fe and stretches west into Arizona, covering roughly one-third of the state. The Rio Grande flows from the north through the Basin and Range and exits New Mexico in the south near Las Cruces, forming the border between Texas and Mexico. This region is marked by rugged mountain ranges, including the Guadalupe, Sacramento, and San Andres ranges. **Desert basins** are situated between the ranges.

NEW MEXICO'S CLIMATE

Climate is measured by three factors: the amount of **precipitation,** the pattern of temperatures in the state, and the direction and power of the wind.

The mountains slow or trap clouds. Consequently, the area to the east of the mountains receives little or no rain.

Generally, the state has a warm, dry climate. Afternoon rainstorms usually pass quickly. In the mountains, as much as 300 inches of snow can fall during the winter. The town of Chama in the northern part of New Mexico receives an average of 100 inches of snow during the winter. In contrast, Las Cruces receives about four inches of snow annually.

INFLUENCE OF THE MOUNTAINS

The **altitude** in New Mexico varies from 3,000 feet above sea level in the basins to more than 13,000 feet above sea level in the Rockies. As a result, the state's temperatures also vary. In the summer the town of

Deming in the southern desert averages a monthly high of 94°F, while the northern mountains average a high of 81°F. In the winter, the southeastern town of Roswell has an average minimum temperature of 24°F, while the northern city of Taos has an average minimum temperature of less than 10°F.

The three distinct geographic regions of New Mexico have different climates. It is common for the summer temperatures in the desert and the Great Plains areas to rise higher than 100°F. The mountains are cooler because of their elevation.

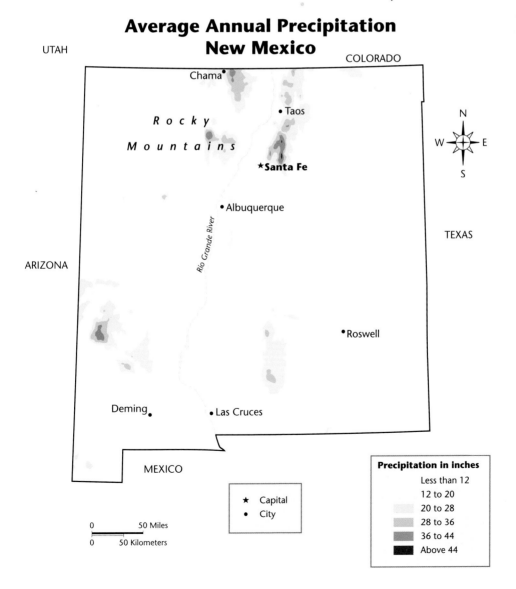

Average Annual Precipitation
New Mexico

UTAH

COLORADO

Chama

Taos

R o c k y

M o u n t a i n s

★Santa Fe

• Albuquerque

Rio Grande River

ARIZONA

TEXAS

•Roswell

Deming.

• Las Cruces

MEXICO

Precipitation in inches
Less than 12
12 to 20
20 to 28
28 to 36
36 to 44
Above 44

★ Capital
• City

0   50 Miles

0   50 Kilometers

Famous Firsts

FAMOUS FIRSTS BEFORE STATEHOOD

In August 1680 the Pueblo started the first successful revolt of Native Americans against the Spanish invaders. After a deadly nine-day battle in which the Pueblo burned down present-day Santa Fe, the Spanish retreated to an area called El Paso del Norte, which is now Juarez, Mexico.

In 1712 Santa Fe began a yearly celebration, marking the return of the Spanish to the city and the defeat of the Pueblo. Every September since then, the city has staged a citywide party called La Fiesta de Santa Fe. It is now the oldest continually observed event in the United States.

In 1898 Thomas Alva Edison, the inventor of the light bulb and phonograph, filmed the world's first movie in New Mexico. Called *Indian Day School,* the movie was a 50-second documentary that began by showing the doorway of a building and a sign identifying it as the Isleta Indian School in Isleta, New Mexico. A moment later,

La Fiesta de Santa Fe has been an annual event for nearly 300 years. Parades, dances, and concerts are just a few of the events that attract locals and tourists.

children come out of the door and pass in front of the camera. When it was shown around the country, it was the first time many people had seen Native Americans.

FAMOUS FIRSTS OF THE 1900'S

In 1924 the Gila Wilderness became the first area in the country to be set aside as a national wilderness site. This means that it is off-limits to roads and buildings, and no one can disturb the land or hunt the animals living there. Logging, mining, resort building, and other businesses are not allowed. The Gila Wilderness is also the nation's largest wilderness site at 3.3 million acres.

From 1943 to 1945 the first atomic bombs were built at a secret laboratory at Los Alamos, in the mountains near Santa Fe. One bomb was tested in a remote desert on July 16, 1945. The other two were dropped on Japanese cities toward the end of **World War II** (1939–1945).

Ground zero of the first atomic bomb test is marked by a memorial statue made of black lava rock. Dropped from a 150 foot tower the bomb exploded at 5:30 am over the New Mexico desert.

New Mexico's State Symbols

NEW MEXICO STATE FLAG

The circle in the middle of the state flag stands for life and love. The four points represent the four directions, the four seasons, the four times of day (sunrise, noon, evening, and night), and the four stages of human life (childhood, youth, adulthood, and old age). Reba Mera, the wife of a Santa Fe doctor and **archaeologist,** designed the flag, which became the official state flag in 1925.

*The New Mexico state flag features a sun symbol based on an **ancient** sun symbol from the Zia Pueblo people. The Zia and other Pueblo tribes are the ancestors of the Anasazi, the first people to live in what is now New Mexico.*

STATE NICKNAME: THE LAND OF ENCHANTMENT

If you see a car with a New Mexico license plate, you may see the phrase "The Land of Enchantment." In 1906 Arthur Rackham, a children's book illustrator, used the phrase as the title for a book. Although the book was not about New Mexico, the phrase was put on license plates in 1941 and became the state nickname in 1999.

The New Mexico state seal is used as a stamp to mark official government papers.

NEW MEXICO STATE SEAL

The state seal of New Mexico features a large bald eagle, which is a symbol for the United States. Using its wings, the bird shelters a smaller Mexican eagle, which shows how New Mexico was once owned by Mexico. The year 1912 is when New Mexico became a state.

STATE MOTTO: *CRESCIT EUNDO*

Most states also have a motto, or a saying that people commonly use to describe the state. New Mexico's state motto uses the Latin words *Crescit eundo,* which means "It grows as it goes." This motto describes how the New Mexicans look to the future as a time of progress.

STATE SONGS: "O, FAIR NEW MEXICO" AND "ASI ES NUEVO MEXICO"

New Mexico has two state songs, one in English and the other in Spanish. Elizabeth Garrett wrote "O, Fair New Mexico" in 1917. Her famous father, Sheriff Pat Garrett,

"O, Fair New Mexico"

Under a sky of azure,
where balmy breezes blow,
Kissed by the golden sunshine,
is Nuevo Mejico.
Land of the Montezuma,
with fiery hearts aglow,
Land of the deeds historic,
is Nuevo Mejico.

Chorus
O, fair New Mexico, we love,
we love you so,
Our hearts with pride o'erflow,
No matter where we go.
O, fair New Mexico, we love,
we love you so,
The grandest state we know
—New Mexico!

Native Americans often used the yucca plant for food and to make soaps and shampoo. They also wove baskets from its leaves.

killed the outlaw Billy the Kid in 1881. In 1928 the famous composer John Philip Sousa added the music. Amadeo Lucero wrote *"Asi Es Nuevo Mexico"* and played his song on guitar in front of the state legislature in 1971. Soon after, it was selected as the Spanish-language state song.

STATE FLOWER: YUCCA

The yucca was chosen as the state flower by New Mexico schoolchildren in 1927. The yucca is a large plant that grows in many parts of the state. It has spiky green leaves at its base and waxy white flowers on top.

STATE TREE: PIÑON

Piñon forests cover one-quarter of New Mexico. So it is not surprising that the state **legislature** selected the piñon as the state tree in 1948. It is a member of the pine tree family, growing as tall as fifteen feet.

STATE BIRD: ROADRUNNER

Early settlers in New Mexico noticed a special kind of bird that could run very fast,

The piñon tree produces pinecones that contain piñon nuts, which are used in New Mexican foods. The wood has a fragrant smell when burned in fireplaces.

Roadrunners actually can fly, but they seem to prefer to run. They can run as fast as twenty miles per hour.

often in the tracks made by wagon wheels. This gave the settlers the idea of calling them roadrunners. In 1932 citizens voted to make the long-tailed, light brown and white birds the official state bird.

STATE MAMMAL: BLACK BEAR

The state mammal is the black bear. This animal was chosen in 1963 to honor a black bear that survived a forest fire in 1950 in the Capitan Mountains of south-central New Mexico. The forest service workers who rescued the bear named him Smokey Bear. The U.S. Forest Service used him as a symbol to teach generations of children about fire safety in the national forests.

Black bears may not always be black. They can be brown or reddish brown. They live in the mountains and forests. Adults can weigh up to 600 pounds.

STATE FOSSIL: COELOPHYSIS

Coelophysis fossils were first discovered by David Baldwin in 1881, at Ghost Ranch in northern New Mexico. This dinosaur lived more than 200 million years ago and was one of the earliest dinosaurs. The coelophysis was a meat eater with a toothy jaw that was used to tear the flesh of its prey. More than a thousand fossils have been dug up in the Ghost Ranch area. In 1981 the coelophysis was named the state fossil.

The coelophysis was nine feet long and walked on two legs.

The New Mexico cutthroat trout lives in the cold waters of mountain lakes.

STATE FISH: NEW MEXICO CUTTHROAT TROUT

The New Mexico cutthroat trout was given its name because of the distinct red stripes under its throat. It became the state fish in 1955. It takes about four years for the cutthroat trout to mature enough to produce offspring. This species was in danger because its **habitat** was being destroyed and there was competition from other trout introduced to its home waters. However, the state now protects this trout and has breeding programs to increase its numbers.

STATE INSECT: TARANTULA HAWK WASP

In 1989 New Mexico chose the tarantula hawk wasp as its state insect. Its favorite food is the tarantula spider. The wasp stings a tarantula, which paralyzes it. The wasp then drags the paralyzed spider to its nest and lays eggs on it. The hatched eggs, or larvae, feed on the living spider until they are strong enough to leave the nest.

The tarantula hawk wasp is from the wasp family. It is named after a hawk because it can swoop down like one to find food.

The state legislature chose turquoise as the state gem in 1967.

STATE GEM: TURQUOISE

Turquoise represents an important piece of New Mexico history. Settlers who came looking for gold in the 1800s discovered blue and green rocks in the central area of the state. The gems became so sought after that the busy trail to this part of the state was called the Turquoise Trail. Native Americans use turquoise in their traditional jewelry.

STATE COOKIE: BIZCOHCITO

The bizcohcito is a small sugar cookie flavored with a spice called anise, which comes from the seeds of a plant that grows in New Mexico. Anise tastes like black licorice and makes the cookies spicy and sweet. The recipe has been handed down by generations of Hispanic families in southern New Mexico.

Chosen as the state cookie in 1989, bizcohcito is sweet and spicy.

New Mexico's History and People

New Mexico's recorded history dates back to the mid-1500s. Few states have longer histories.

First Inhabitants

Most scientists believe that the first people to live in North America came from Asia. Some of these people settled in the present-day Southwest, perhaps as long ago as 15,000 years ago. From around 800 to 1300, hunters and farmers called these people the Anasazi, meaning "ancient ones" in the Navajo language. The Pueblo tribes descended from the Anasazi.

The Anasazi are best known for building large villages out of adobe, or sun-baked clay. These special structures are called pueblos. No one is quite sure why, but the Anasazi people eventually left their pueblos in about 1300 and moved to other areas. Scientists believe that a **drought** may have been the reason.

Built in the 900s, Pueblo Bonito has about 800 rooms and 32 underground chambers.

Thousands of pueblo ruins have been found in New Mexico and Arizona. One of the most famous Anasazi sites is Pueblo Bonito, in northwestern New Mexico. The **descendants** of the Anasazi people formed living groups, each with its own language and customs. These tribes include the Zuni, Santo Domingo, Acoma, Laguna, Isleta, Taos, Cochiti, Zia, and others.

EARLY SPANISH EXPLORERS

By the early 1500s European explorers from Spain crossed the Atlantic Ocean and conquered Mexico. They made their way north to present-day New Mexico. These explorers wanted to bring back gold for their king. The Spanish invaders also believed that all Native Americans should become Roman Catholic, the official religion of Spain. As a result, they forced Native Americans to practice Roman Catholicism. The Spanish remained in control of present-day New Mexico until the 1800s.

ANGLO EXPLORERS

By the early 1800s the West began to interest explorers in the United States. In 1806 U.S. army officer Zebulon Pike

Zebulon Pike's expedition to explore the western Great Plains and Rocky Mountains led to his discovery of Pike's Peak in Colorado.

Esteban and the Search for Gold

Esteban, or Estevancio de Dorantes, was a black explorer from Morocco, in North Africa. In 1539 he became a guide for the Spanish, leading them to New Mexico in search of gold. As his party approached the small Zuni town of Hawikuh, near present-day Gallup, they believed they saw a huge amount of gold glittering in the distance, and they attacked the Zuni. In defense the Zuni killed Esteban and many other members of his group. The gold was the sun reflecting off nearby tall grasses or wheat.

was sent by President Thomas Jefferson to explore the western territory, and he reached what is present-day northern New Mexico. The Spanish settlers, however, did not want Americans on their land. Spanish soldiers forced Pike to leave, so he returned to his base in Louisiana.

THE SANTA FE TRAIL

In 1810 Mexicans, demanding their freedom from Spain, began a war of independence that lasted more than ten years. On September 27, 1821, representatives of the Spanish crown and the Mexican rebels signed the Treaty of Córdoba, which recognized Mexican independence. This meant that New Mexico was now ruled by Mexico. Mexico was eager to exchange goods with the United States. A year after Mexico's independence, a trader named William Becknell traveled from his home in Missouri to Santa Fe. He brought knives, cooking pots, cloth, clocks, and mirrors, which he traded with the New Mexicans for gold, silver, fur, and leather. The trip was so successful that many people began making the journey to trade goods. The well-traveled path became known as the Santa Fe Trail.

Claiming New Mexico for the United States, General Stephen Kearny raised a U.S. flag and then named himself the first governor of the territory.

THE WAR WITH MEXICO

Since Mexican independence in 1821, the territory of Texas had been part of Mexico. In 1836 Texas declared itself an independent country. Mexico fought a long war with the **Anglo** settlers who had settled Texas and founded it as a new nation. In 1846 the United States admitted Texas as a new U.S. territory and began to fight Mexico for the land. In the end, the United States would win Texas and other lands from Mexico. Also during that war, General Stephen Kearny marched into Santa Fe in 1896 and claimed it for the United States during the war.

In 1853 the United States bought from the Mexican government the land that makes up the extreme southern corner of New Mexico. The United States paid $10 million for about 30,000 square miles. It is called the Gadsden Purchase because James Gadsden, an army officer who was the U.S. minister to Mexico at the time, arranged it.

GROWTH OF THE NEW MEXICO TERRITORY

After the **Civil War** (1861–1865) and the completion of a coast-to-coast railroad in 1896, the western United States grew quickly. In 1863 New Mexico became a territory. The Navajo and the Apache tribes lost much of their farmland to Anglo settlers. A period of bloody conflict began in 1860, which historians call the Indian Wars. It ended in 1890 with the defeat of the Lakota at Wounded Knee in present-day Montana.

In 1864 the U.S. Army, led by Colonel Kit Carson, forced the Navajos to move to a **reservation** in east-central New Mexico. This ordeal became known as the Long Walk. About 200 Navajo died of starvation and illness during the relocation. The Apache did not go without a struggle. Led by their warrior chief Geronimo, they fought the U.S. Army until 1868, when soldiers captured him. Geronimo's arrest marked the end of the Indian Wars.

One cause of the Indian Wars was the expansion of the railroad, which cut across

Geronimo was born in 1829 in what is today western New Mexico, but was then still Mexican territory.

Navajo and Apache settlements. Not only did settlers fight the Native Americans but they also fought among themselves for control of state land and natural resources. These conflicts from 1878 to 1881 became known as the Lincoln County War.

STATEHOOD

In 1906 the people of present-day New Mexico and Arizona considered becoming a state together. New Mexicans voted in favor of this idea, but Arizona residents did not. Consequently, the leaders of the New Mexico territory met in 1910 and wrote their own constitution to prepare for statehood. The constitution set up a state government and defined rights to its citizens. In 1912 President William H. Taft approved the **petition** sent by New Mexico's citizens asking that New Mexico become a state. On January 6, the U.S. Congress named New Mexico the 47th state. More than 327,000 New Mexico residents became U.S. citizens.

FAMOUS PEOPLE

Mangas Coloradas (mid-1790s–1863), Apache leader. Born in present-day southern Mexico, his name is Spanish for "red sleeves." He brought various Native American tribes together, leading battles against settlers trying to take Native American land.

Conrad Hilton (1887–1979), hotel owner. Born in San Antonio, New Mexico, Hilton became a businessperson after serving in the state's first

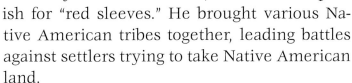

Conrad Hilton was born in a primitive adobe dwelling on Christmas day. When he died at the age of ninety-one he controlled the largest hotel organization in the world.

Navajo Code Talkers in World War II

During **World War II** (1939–1945), the U.S. military used secret codes to try to hide their plans from the Germans and Japanese. However, many of these codes were solved by the enemy. Philip Johnston, who grew up on a Navajo reservation, developed an idea to help the military. He spoke the Navajo language and knew how unique it was. It did not have an alphabet,  was not a written language, and was understood by few people. A group of Navajo men volunteered to use their language to help the U.S. military create an unbreakable code. Afterward, 420 Navajos joined the marines fighting in the Pacific and became known as code talkers.

legislature and fighting in **World War I** (1914–1918). The first hotel to carry the Hilton name was built in Dallas, Texas in 1925. In 1943 Hilton became the first coast-to-coast hotel chain in the United States.

William Hanna (1910–2001), animator. Born in Melrose, Hanna went to Hollywood and worked at MGM Studios as a cartoonist, drawing popular characters such as Tom and Jerry. With partner Joseph Barbera, he formed Hanna-Barbera Productions, which created *Yogi Bear.*

Bill Mauldin (1921–2003), cartoonist and journalist. Born in Mountain Park, he learned to draw cartoons during a long childhood illness. When he joined the army during World War II, he created a cartoon series about the day-to-day life of soldiers Willie and Joe. Later, he won two **Pulitzer Prizes** for his editorial cartoons.

Bill Mauldin became famous by drawing and writing a series of cartoons about U.S. soldiers serving in Europe during World War II.

Bobby Unser (1934–   ) and **Al Unser** (1939–   ), race-car drivers. Born in Albuquerque, the Unser brothers were born to race. Al won the Indianapolis 500 four times (1970, 1971, 1978, 1987), and Bobby won it three times (1968, 1975, 1981).

Linda Wertheimer (1943–   ), radio journalist. Born in Carlsbad, she is best known as a correspondent for *All Things Considered,* the National Public Radio daily news show. In 2001 *All Things Considered* had ten million listeners, making it one of the top five radio shows in the United States.

Sid Gutierrez (1951–   ), astronaut. Growing up in Albuquerque in the early 1950s, Gutierrez dreamed of traveling in space. In June 1991 he did just that. He became the first Hispanic American to pilot the space shuttle. The nine-day mission conducted science experiments to determine how humans and animals adapt to life in space. In 1994 he went on a second mission dedicated to mapping the earth's oceans and land. The mission collected enough information to fill 26,000 encyclopedias.

Nancy Lopez (1957–   ), pro golfer. Born in California, Lopez grew up in Roswell. She won the New Mexico Women's Amateur Golf Tournament at age twelve. Nancy joined the boys' golf team at Goddard High and helped it win two state championships. She turned professional in 1977 and finished second in her first three tournaments. She won the Ladies Professional Golf Association (LPGA) Championship in 1978, 1985, and 1989. At age 35 she became the youngest person ever voted into the LPGA Hall of Fame.

Astronaut Sid Gutierrez has spent twenty days living and working in space.

The Arts of New Mexico

Like its history, New Mexico's arts combine Native American, Hispanic, and **Anglo** traditions. Artists and art lovers are attracted to many galleries and theaters in Santa Fe and Taos.

NATIVE AMERICAN ARTISTS

Navajo artist R. C. Gorman, born in 1932 in Canyon de Chelly, Arizona, discovered his talent early in life. As a boy, he used sand and rocks to paint on the dirt floor of his hogan, which is a Navajo dwelling. He attended college in Mexico City. In 1968 he moved to Taos, where he still lives today. He has created sculptures, ceramics, and tapestries, in addition to paintings. He is especially known for painting Native American women as soft and round. People from all over the world buy and collect Gorman's art.

Mogollon culture first introduced pottery into the land of New Mexico in the 300s.

The famous potter Maria Martinez (1887–1980) lived on the San Ildefonso Pueblo outside of Santa Fe. As a girl, she learned how to make pottery by watching her aunts. She was fascinated by the way a simple lump of clay could be

Today, Georgia O'Keeffe's home is listed on the register of National Historic Places.

made into a bowl or vase. After she married, she and her husband, Julian, began working together to create their special black pottery with painted designs based on ancient patterns found by **archaeologists.** Art historians credit Martinez for helping to keep the art of her **ancestors** alive today for all to enjoy.

SOUTHWESTERN STYLE

Another famous painter with strong ties to New Mexico is Georgia O'Keeffe. Although she was born in Wisconsin in 1887, she spent the last 40 years of her life in Abiquiu, a small village near Taos. She eventually bought a large home there, called Ghost Ranch. Her paintings of cattle skulls and New Mexican landscapes are in museums around the world.

Some of Georgia O'Keeffe's most famous paintings feature the stark southwestern scenery, such as an adobe building, the mountains rising from the desert, or the faded bones of cattle.

New Mexico's State Government

Government comes from the word "govern," which means to guide and protect. While the U.S. government is responsible for running the entire nation, each state has its own government. Like the U.S. government, New Mexico's government is made up of three different branches that work together to run the state: the legislative, the executive, and the judicial. The New Mexico state constitution is the only one in the United States

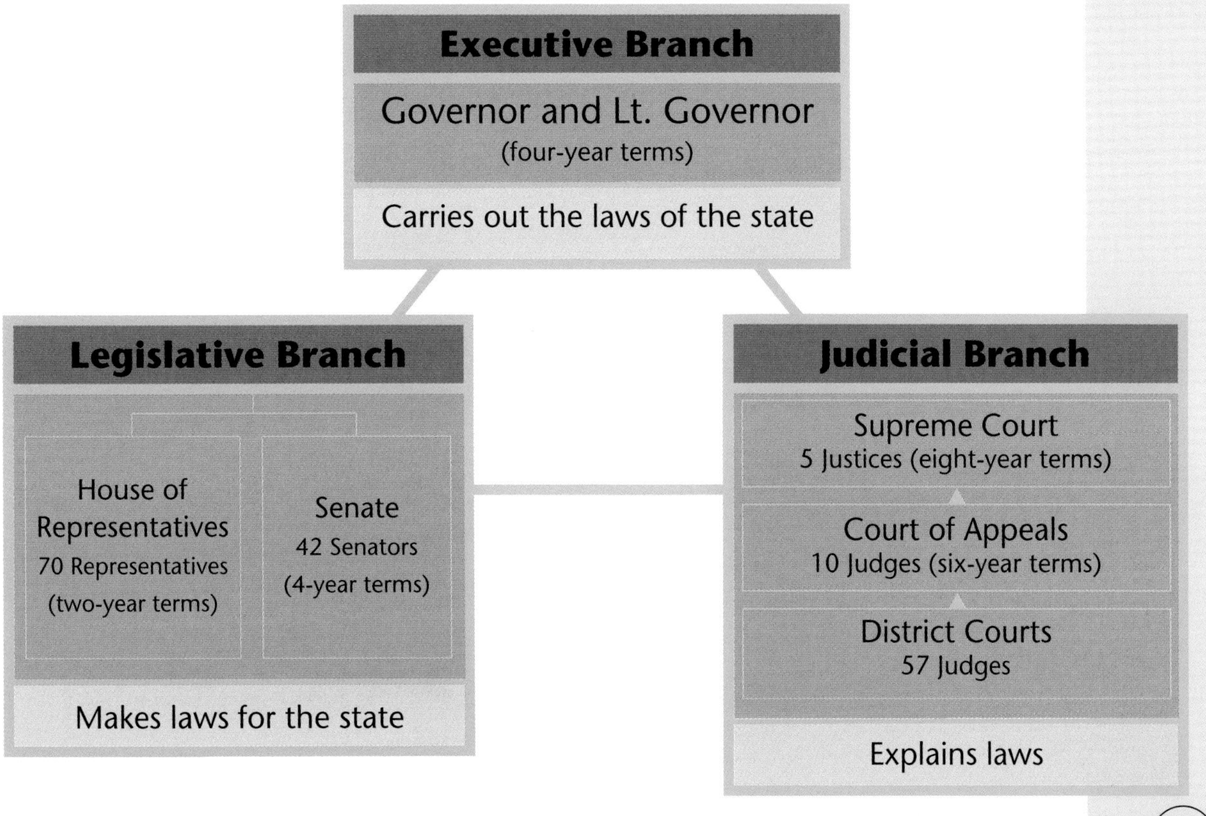

Executive Branch

Governor and Lt. Governor
(four-year terms)

Carries out the laws of the state

Legislative Branch

House of Representatives
70 Representatives
(two-year terms)

Senate
42 Senators
(4-year terms)

Makes laws for the state

Judicial Branch

Supreme Court
5 Justices (eight-year terms)

Court of Appeals
10 Judges (six-year terms)

District Courts
57 Judges

Explains laws

The N.M. capitol is shaped like the zia sun symbol, the official emblem of New Mexico

that lists Spanish and English as official state languages. This is because 40 percent of the population is Hispanic.

LEGISLATIVE BRANCH

The legislative branch of New Mexico's government is responsible for proposing new laws and sending them to the governor for his or her approval. In addition, the legislature is responsible for creating a state budget and deciding how New Mexico will spend its money. The **legislature** is divided into two groups. The larger group is the house of representatives, with 70 members. Each representative serves a two-year term. The smaller group is the senate, with 42 senators. They each serve a four-year term.

EXECUTIVE BRANCH

The executive branch carries out the laws of the state. The head of the executive branch is the governor. He or she is elected to a four-year term by New Mexico voters. Helping the governor is the lieutenant or assistant governor, the **attorney** general, state treasurer, secretary of state, and other department heads.

JUDICIAL BRANCH

In New Mexico the judicial branch of government interprets the state's laws and applies them in real situations. District courts have 57 judges, located in cities all over New Mexico. These women and men listen to the cases of local citizens. Some cases involve criminal acts, such

Palace of the Governors

The Palace of the Governors is the oldest public building in the United States. Spanish settlers built it in 1609, when the city of Santa Fe was founded. It became the official residence of Spanish, Mexican, and then U.S. governors until 1907. It is now a museum with exhibits on early life in the Santa Fe area. The building is nicknamed the "Round House" because its shape resembles a **kiva,** which is a special round-shaped room where sacred Pueblo ceremonies take place.

as robbery or murder. Others, called civil cases, are about business or family disputes.

Above the district courts is the court of appeals. Here, ten judges listen to legal cases from lower courts, to be sure that everything was handled according to the law.

Five justices, appointed by the governor and approved by the state senate, make up the supreme court, the highest court in New Mexico. They serve eight years. The supreme court is the final authority on state law, and it also hears cases involving the U.S. Constitution and New Mexico.

In addition to this court system, many Native American **reservations** in New Mexico have their own system of rules called Tribal Law. Although they must still follow the laws of the state, the leaders of a reservation may sometimes decide on the fairness of a certain village issue, such as a business dispute.

New Mexico's Culture

Many different cultures blend together to make New Mexico a unique place. Native Americans, Hispanic Americans, and white Americans are the three largest groups in the state. Small numbers of African Americans and Asian Americans also call New Mexico home. Living side by side, these cultures share their special customs, music, food, religions, language, and art.

A BLENDING OF CULTURES

In New Mexico one of every ten citizens is a Native American. This is the highest percentage of Native Americans in all of the 50 states. New Mexico's Pueblo, Navajo, and Zuni can trace their roots back to the earliest ancestors of the Southwest. The largest Native American nation in New Mexico is the Navajo.

A pueblo has rooms that connect to one another and may hold as many as 100 people. Several stories high, the dwellings are entered by a ladder, which can be pulled inside to prevent outsiders from entering.

After Native Americans, Hispanic Americans have the longest history of living in the Southwest, almost 500 years.

The U.S. cowboy has long symbolized the West. As settlers moved west, cowboys and cowgirls developed special skills. At a New Mexico rodeo, an audience can watch Hispanic, Anglo, and Native American cowboys and cowgirls ride broncos and bulls, rope running calves, and race trained horses around barrels.

A New Mexico rodeo showcases modern cowboys and cowgirls competing in events that originated on cattle ranches.

INDIAN MARKET

At the end of the summer, Santa Fe gears up for its yearly Indian Market. More than 1,200 individual artists representing 100 Native American tribes showcase their wares.

In Hatch, on Labor Day each year, is the Hatch Chili Festival. Hatch, known as the "Chili Capital of the World," develops new varieties of chilies.

New Mexico's Art Fairs

Because the weather is so mild during New Mexico's summers, several large art festivals are held outdoors. The New Mexico Arts and Crafts Fair is sponsored by the city of Albuquerque and began in 1962. Today, more than 220 New Mexico artists and craftspeople gather to display and sell their pottery, weavings, paintings, and jewelry.

New Mexico's Food

The traditional foods of New Mexico are based around a few main ingredients, such as meat, beans, chili peppers, corn, tortillas, and lots of spices.

SOUTHWESTERN CUISINE

Many New Mexicans like foods that are spicy and hot as fire. Among some commonly used spices are cumin, anise, cilantro, and oregano.

The most popular kind of spice in New Mexico comes from chili peppers. The state grows more of these red and green pods than any other state—more than 60 percent of all chili peppers in the nation. Just a few of the many kinds are New Mexico, Anaheim, poblano, serrano, jalapeño, and habanero. Green chili peppers are usually roasted and peeled. Red chili comes from green peppers that have ripened and dried.

Corn is also an important food in New Mexico. For thousands of years, it was the mainstay of the Native American diet. Corn can be roasted over a fire, baked in an oven, and made into a soup, stew, or sauce. Hominy, or dried corn kernels, is often used as

The hot and spicy taste of red chili peppers will vary depending on the shade of red. The darker the red of the chili, the more spicy it will be.

Cornmeal Pancakes

Be sure to have an adult help you make this simple yet tasty New Mexican favorite.

Ingredients

1 cup white or yellow cornmeal

1 tablespoon honey

1 teaspoon salt

1 cup boiling water

½ cup all-purpose flour

2 teaspoons baking powder

1 large egg

½ cup evaporated milk

Directions

1. Combine the first three ingredients in a medium-size bowl. Slowly stir in the boiling water. Cover the bowl and let stand for 10 minutes.
2. Stir in the flour and baking powder.
3. Mix the egg and evaporated milk together in another bowl and add to the cornmeal mixture.
4. Spoon about ¼ cup batter for each pancake onto a heated, lightly greased griddle or skillet.
5. Cook for about 1 minute or until bubbles appear, then turn and cook on the other side until golden.
6. Serve warm with butter, syrup, jam, or other topping.

the base for many dishes. Once corn is cooked, it also can be ground into meal and made into tortillas, round pieces of flat bread. Native Americans of the Southwest have been making tortillas for centuries. Tortillas can be filled with beans, cooked meats, and vegetables, and become tacos, burritos, or **quesadillas.** They can be eaten plain, like bread, and used to scoop up extra sauce.

New Mexico's Folklore and Legends

A legend is an exciting story about people or events that gets handed down from generation to generation. Often, each teller of the story adds a new detail, straight from his or her imagination. This is why there may be many different versions of the same basic story. Folklore is a name given to simple stories from long ago that try to explain complicated things.

PECOS BILL

In New Mexico there are many legends about Pecos Bill. He was a made-up cowboy created by other cowboys to pass the time around the campfire at night. According to the many tall tales, Pecos Bill was raised by coyotes and could ride any animal on earth. He could do rope tricks, brand cattle, and fight the meanest enemy.

PECOS BILL FINDS A HARD OUTFIT

In this popular legend, Pecos Bill wants to find a group of tough men to work with. He sets off on his horse and soon meets a rattlesnake. He scares the big snake and then wraps it around his neck. Next, he meets a fierce cougar. He quickly tames the cougar, puts his saddle on it, and rides it into town. When the tough guys at the local saloon see Pecos Bill riding a cougar with a snake around his neck, they call him "boss" right away!

THE ANASAZI DISAPPEAR

The Anasazi mysteriously disappeared from New Mexico around 500 years ago after creating a productive and powerful society. According to this story, the Anasazi offended the great spirits by performing a sacred healing ceremony. They were warned four times by the spirits not to perform the ceremony. However, the Anasazi did not listen. On the fifth day, a huge wind blew all the people from their land and tossed them around the countryside. The Anasazi never came back together. They left their dwellings behind as a reminder to listen to the great spirits.

UFOS—FACT OR FOLKLORE?

A more modern legend concerns aliens, spaceships, and Roswell, New Mexico. In 1947 a group of people claimed to have seen a UFO—unidentified flying object—land in the desert. They were sure they saw the bodies of three dead aliens. State officials said it was a weather balloon that had crashed. However, the people of Roswell refused to believe this. They began to develop spaceship fever. Newspapers could not get enough of these stories. Many people began to visit Roswell, looking for aliens. Some claimed to see mysterious things. Today, people still come to Roswell to try to spot a flying saucer. They also visit the International UFO Museum and Research Center and the UFO Enigma Museum. The Enigma Museum features a plastic model of an alien and items from science fiction movies.

New Mexico's Sports Teams

Like other states with small populations, New Mexico does not have major professional baseball, football, basketball, and hockey teams. But, there is still plenty of local sports action to satisfy fans.

COLLEGE SPORTS

The University of New Mexico sports teams are called the Lobos, the Spanish name for wolves. The New Mexico State University teams are called the Aggies because the school began as a place for people to study agriculture. The Western New Mexico University calls its teams the Mustangs, after the wild horses that still roam the area.

The Lobos play their basketball games in an Albuquerque arena nicknamed "The Pit," which *Sports Illustrated* selected as one of the top twenty college arenas in 1999. Several professional stars have played for the Lobos. Michael Cooper, a member of the world champion Los Angeles Lakers in the 1980s and WNBA head coach, was a star for the Lobos. Seven-foot Australian Luc Longley, who played on the world champion Chicago Bulls in

The University of New Mexico men's basketball team recently celebrated its 100th anniversary.

the 1990s alongside Michael Jordan, also played for the Lobos. Lobos fans still remember Marvin "Automatic" Johnson, who set a single-game scoring record of 50 points during a game in 1978. The Lobos also have produced such football stars as Brian Urlacher of the Chicago Bears.

The University of New Mexico women's golf team won four consecutive Mountain West titles from 2000 to 2003.

The University of New Mexico has one of the best women's golf teams in the country. In 2002 the LPGA selected the team's coach, Jackie Booth, as Coach of the Year.

The university has a winning ski team, with talented men and women racers. In 2003 the Lobos finished in the top five at the National Collegiate Athletic Association (NCAA) championships for the fifth straight year. In 2002 the women skiers were the national champions in the **slalom** event.

MINOR LEAGUE BASEBALL

Albuquerque's baseball history stretches back more than 100 years, and there have been many teams. For example, the Albuquerque Dukes, which left the city in 2001, played there for more than 40 years. Such major league stars as Pedro Martinez, Raul Mondesi, and Mike Piazza played for the Dukes. In 2003 baseball returned to Albuquerque with the Albuquerque **Isotopes** of the Pacific Coast League. They are **affiliated** with Major League Baseball's Florida Marlins, who won the 2003 World Series.

New Mexico's Businesses and Products

New Mexico has long been a place where great discoveries are made. Today, those great discoveries contribute to the wealth of the state along side of more traditional industries like mining and farming.

LOS ALAMOS SCIENTIFIC LABORATORY

Founded in the early 1940s to build the first atomic bomb, Los Alamos remains one of the nation's top research labs, particularly in its study of the **atom.** The center attracts scientists and students from around the world. It also plays an important role in New Mexico's economy, contributing $4.9 billion each year

Los Alamos National Laboratory is the largest employer in Northern New Mexico with more than 10,000 employees

Chili peppers grow well in hot, dry conditions, which explains why so many are grown in New Mexico.

because so many people work at the lab and the lab's discoveries are used around the world.

FARM PRODUCTS

Agriculture has long been important to New Mexico's economy. The livestock industry is particularly important. In fact, New Mexico has more cattle and sheep than it has people. New Mexico is the country's leading producer of chilies and summer onions.

TOURISM

More than four million people visited New Mexico in 2000. With fourteen national parks and monuments and five national forests, the great outdoors draws a crowd all year long.

MINING

The mining industry also is important to New Mexico. New Mexico ranks second in the nation for uranium and copper production. Uranium is especially important because it is used to make nuclear energy. Copper is used to make plumbing pipe and pennies. Potash mining boomed in the 1930s. Potash is used in fertilizer, and New Mexico leads the country in potash production.

Attractions and Landmarks

New Mexico attracts millions of people each year who come to enjoy its beauty, cultural and historical attractions, and recreational activities.

NATURAL ATTRACTIONS

Carlsbad Caverns National Park is a huge underground maze of rooms and tunnels that were created as water carved away layers of limestone over millions of years. The cave rooms, or caverns, are filled with **stalagmites** and **stalactites.** Many rooms have unusual names such as "Whale's Mouth" and "Hall of the Giants." The biggest

Carlsbad Caverns was declared a national park in 1930.

Places to See in New Mexico

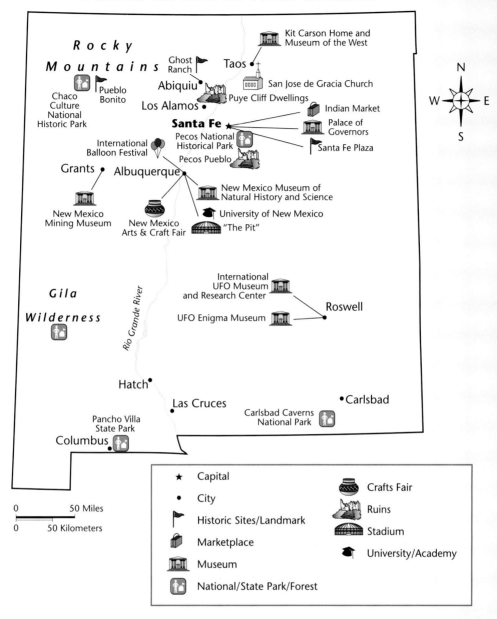

cavern, called the "Big Room," is so large that it can hold fourteen football fields. Visitors are not allowed in certain caves. This rule helps protect nesting Mexican free-tailed bats.

MUSEUMS AND BUILDINGS

Outside of Santa Fe are the Puye Cliff Dwellings. These well-preserved ruins were built into a cliff face. Historians

The Spanish explorer Coronado wrote about the Pecos Pueblo in 1540 and said, "It is feared through the land." Pecos was the largest pueblo with more than 2,000 people and 500 warriors.

believe Native Americans lived in these dwellings between 1200 and the late 1500s. Visitors use stone steps and wooden ladders to move among the nearly 600 rooms.

The Pecos Pueblo is located in Pecos National Historical Park, fifteen miles northwest of Santa Fe. The site is the ruins of a pueblo built in the 1400s that once had 660 rooms and dozens of **kivas.** The Spanish built a church here that served as a mission. The visitors' center has displays of the history of the Pecos people.

The Santa Fe Plaza is a square in the center of the oldest part of the city. Surrounded by shops, restaurants, art galleries, and historic landmarks, it is truly the heart of Santa Fe. It was an active place of trading between people as

Santa Fe Plaza has been the commercial, social, and political center of Santa Fe since 1610 when it was established by the explorer Don Pedro de Peralta.

General Francisco "Pancho" Villa and General John J. Pershing

Some people consider Pancho Villa an outlaw. Others consider him a hero, fighting to free Mexico from its strong neighbor to the north, the United States. What historians agree on is that in the early morning darkness of March 9, 1916, Villa crossed from Mexico into southern New Mexico. He then attacked the village of Columbus, leaving it a smoking ruin. A week later, the U.S. Army crossed into Mexico, traveling hundreds of miles in search of Villa. The troops were led by General John "Black Jack" Pershing. Pershing's men spent eleven months chasing Villa, but they never caught him. Because of his fearless ability to elude the U.S. Army, Pancho Villa remains a Mexican folk hero.

far back as 1610, ten years before the Pilgrims landed at Plymouth Rock.

Located between Taos and Santa Fe, the San Jose de Gracia Church was built between 1770 and 1776. The church is one of the best-preserved examples of Spanish colonial architecture. It has a tile roof supported by wooden beams and walls of white adobe.

In southern New Mexico, visitors can see the village of Columbus and Camp Furlong. It was here in 1916 that the famous Mexican bandit Pancho Villa invaded the United States, killing ten civilians and eight soldiers. It is now the site of Pancho Villa State Park.

NEW MEXICO MINING MUSEUM

The New Mexico Mining Museum in Grants offers self-guided tours that allow visitors to see the equipment and special clothing that miners wear, including protective overalls and breathing gear. They also can view photographs of miners at work. To get a real taste of mining, visitors can take a ride in the "cage," or open elevator,

Kit Carson Home and Museum of the West

The Kit Carson Home is in Taos, a block away from the main plaza. Now the only general history museum in Taos, the house once belonged to the trapper and mountain guide Kit Carson. As an army officer, Carson led many military battles against Native Americans. Although he never learned to read or write, he dictated his many adventure stories to a friend. Consequently, his legend lives on. The house's living room, bedroom, and kitchen are furnished the way they might have been during Carson's time. The furniture includes a wood-burning stove and oven, beds covered with quilts, and handmade dressers, chairs, and tables. Carson lived there from 1843 until his death in 1868.

down to Section 26 of a nonactive uranium mine. There, visitors will learn all about drilling, blasting, and other mining tasks. Displays in the museum show the history of mining in New Mexico and how uranium mining contributed to the state's growth.

Many of the old shacks where miners lived are now historic landmarks used to educate the public and memorialize the sacrifices of the mining industry.

Map of New Mexico

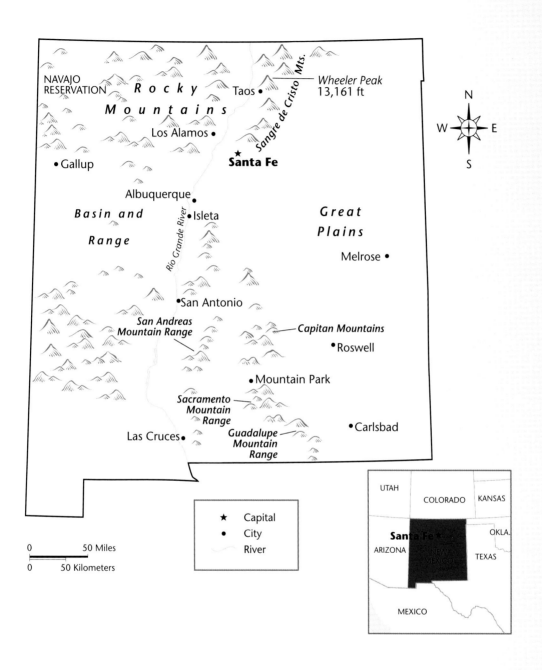

NAVAJO
RESERVATION

Rocky
Mountains

Taos •

Wheeler Peak
13,161 ft

Sangre de Cristo Mts.

Los Alamos •

• Gallup

★
Santa Fe

Albuquerque •
• Isleta

Basin and

Range

Rio Grande River

Great
Plains

Melrose •

•San Antonio

San Andreas
Mountain Range

Capitan Mountains

• Roswell

• Mountain Park

Sacramento
Mountain
Range

Las Cruces •

Guadalupe
Mountain
Range

• Carlsbad

★   Capital
•   City
～ River

0   50 Miles

0   50 Kilometers

UTAH
COLORADO   KANSAS
Santa Fe ★
OKLA.
ARIZONA   NEW
MEXICO   TEXAS
MEXICO

Glossary

affiliated to associate or join with a larger or more important body

altitude the height of a place or thing measured from sea level. With an altitude of 7,000 feet, Santa Fe is the highest state capital.

ancestors people from the past to whom you are related, such as grandparents

ancient long ago or very old

Anglo a white resident of the United States who is not of Hispanic descent

archaeologist a person who studies the remains of past human activities, such as burials, buildings, tools, and pottery

atom the smallest unit of a piece of matter

attorney a person legally appointed to act as an agent for another

Aztec a member of a Native American tribe from Mexico whose civilization was at its height at the time of the Spanish conquest in the early 16th century

Civil War the war in the United States between the Union and the Confederacy from 1861 to 1865

descendants people tracing their lives back to parents, grandparents, and beyond

desert basin a region drained by a river and the streams that flow into it

drought period of little or no rain

fossils the remains of a plant or animal from a past geologic age that is preserved in rock

habitat the area or natural environment in which an animal or a plant normally lives or grows

isotopes one of two or more forms of an element that may be radioactive

kivas large, underground ceremonial chambers

legislature a body of persons empowered to make and change the laws of a nation or state

petition a formal request from a group of people to its leader or leaders to take a specific action

precipitation water, in the form of rain or snow, that falls from the sky

Pulitzer Prizes awards given each year to the best writers of newspaper articles, books, poetry, and plays

quesadillas a flour tortilla filled with a savory mixture, then folded in half to form a turnover shape

ratio a relation in degree or number between two similar things

reservation place set aside by the government where Native Americans were brought to live

semiarid lacking enough water to support trees; desertlike

slalom the act or sport of skiing in a zigzag manner

stalactites an icicle-shaped collection of minerals hanging from the roof of a cave

stalagmites a cone-shaped collection of minerals rising from the floor of a cave

U.S.–Mexican War a war fought between the United States and Mexico from 1846 to 1848 over possession of Texas and other lands now in the southwestern United States

World War I a war fought from 1914 to 1918, in which Great Britain, France, the United States, and their allies defeated Germany, Austria-Hungary, and their allies

World War II a war fought from 1939 to 1945, in which Great Britain, France, the Soviet Union, the United States, and their allies defeated Germany, Italy, and Japan

More Books to Read

Burgan, Michael. *New Mexico: Land of Enchantment (World Almanac Library of the States)*. New York: World Almanac, 2003

Freedman, Russell. *In the Days of the Vaqueros: America's First True Cowboys*. New York: Clarion Books, 2001.

Keegan, Marcia. *Pueblo Girls: Growing Up in Two Worlds*. Santa Fe, N.M.: Clear Light Publishers, 1999.

Kent, Deborah. *New Mexico (America the Beautiful. Second Series)*. Danbury, Conn.: Children's Press, 1999.

Sherrow, Victoria. *The Making of the Atom Bomb*. San Diego, CA: Lucent Books, 2000.

Index

About the Author

Coleen Hubbard is the author of numerous books for adults and children, including the *Dog Tales* series. She is a frequent visitor to New Mexico and lives in the neighboring state of Colorado.